# ISSUES
## today

A resource for KS3

# Global Climate Change

Editor: **Lisa Firth**

ISSUE
**58**

*Independence*
**Educational Publishers**
Cambridge

First published by Independence

The Studio, High Green, Great Shelford

Cambridge CB22 5EG

England

© Independence 2012

**British Library Cataloguing in Publication Data**

Global climate change – (Issues today; v. 58)

1. Climate changes – Effect of human beings on – Juvenile literature  2. Global warming – Juvenile literature  3. Climate change mitigation – Juvenile literature

I. Series II. Firth, Lisa

368.7'3874-dc23

ISBN-13: 978 1 86168 610 7

# Acknowledgements

The publisher is grateful for permission to reproduce the following material.

While every care has been taken to trace and acknowledge copyright, the publisher tenders its apology for any accidental infringement or where copyright has proved untraceable. The publisher would be pleased to come to a suitable arrangement in any such case with the rightful owner.

Chapter One: Climate Science

*Myths about climate change*, © Crown copyright is reproduced with the permission of Her Majesty's Stationery Office, *What about climate change in the future?*, © National Trust, *Ten facts on climate science*, © Crown copyright is reproduced with the permission of Her Majesty's Stationery Office, *The social and economic impacts of climate change*, © Earthwatch Institute, *Climate change: the forest connection*, © Sinks Watch, *Climate change scepticism*, © YouGov, *Climate change blame?*, © YouGov.

Chapter Two: Climate Solutions

*Adapting to the greenhouse*, © Panos London, *The Kyoto Protocol*, © Crown copyright is reproduced with the permission of Her Majesty's Stationery Office, *Carbon offsets*, © David Suzuki Foundation, *Key agreements in the history of climate change*, © Independence Educational Publishers, *We have to adapt culturally to climate change*, © Dr. Jenny Pickerill.

All illustrations, including the cover, are by Don Hatcher.

Editorial by Carolyn Kirby and layout by Jackie Staines, on behalf of Independence Educational Publishers.

Printed in Great Britain by MWL Print Group Ltd.

Lisa Firth

Cambridge

January 2012

# Issues today

# Global Climate Change

# Contents

# issues today

# A resource for KS3

## About Key Stage 3

Key Stage 3 refers to the first three years of secondary schooling, normally years 7, 8 and 9, during which pupils are aged between 11 and 14.

This series is also suitable for Scottish P7, S1 and S2 students.

## About *Issues Today*

*Issues Today* is a series of resource books on contemporary social issues for Key Stage 3 pupils. It is based on the concept behind the popular *Issues* series for 14- to 18-year-olds, also published by Independence.

Each volume contains information from a variety of sources, including government reports and statistics, newspaper and magazine articles, surveys and polls, academic research and literature from charities and lobby groups. The information has been tailored to an 11 to 14 age group; it has been rewritten and presented in a simple, straightforward format to be accessible to Key Stage 3 pupils.

In addition, each *Issues Today* title features handy tasks and assignments based on the information contained in the book, for use in class, for homework or as a revision aid.

*Issues Today* can be used as a learning resource in a variety of Key Stage 3 subjects, including English, Science, History, Geography, PSHE, Citizenship, Sex and Relationships Education and Religious Education.

## About this book

*Global Climate Change* is the fifty-eighth volume in the *Issues Today* series.

The majority of climate scientists now agree that global warming is occurring at a dangerous rate, mainly as a result of human activity. However, a third of the British public are sceptical as to whether human-induced climate change is really happening. This book examines the issues and debate surrounding global climate change, including how the planet is being affected and what can be done to tackle it.

*Global Climate Change* offers a useful overview of the many issues involved in this topic. However, at the end of each article is a URL for the relevant organisation's website, which can be visited by pupils who want to carry out further research.

Because the information in this book is gathered from a number of different sources, pupils should think about the origin of the text and critically evaluate the information that is presented. Does the source have a particular bias or agenda? Are you being presented with facts or opinions? Do you agree with the writer?

At the end of each chapter there are two pages of activities relating to the articles and issues raised in that chapter. The 'Brainstorm' questions can be done as a group or individually after reading the articles. This should prompt some ideas and lead on to further activities. Some suggestions for such activities are given under the headings 'Oral', 'Moral Dilemmas', 'Research', 'Written' and 'Design' that follow the 'Brainstorm' questions.

For more information about *Issues Today* and its sister series, *Issues* (for pupils aged 14 to 18), please visit the Independence website.

www.independence.co.uk

# Myths about climate change

*CONFUSION AND MYTHS ABOUT CLIMATE CHANGES are widespread.*
*Explore some of the most common misconceptions and the facts behind them.*

## The climate is always changing anyway

The Earth's climate has always changed naturally in the past. But what is happening now is potentially a big change in the Earth's climate, this time caused mainly by human activity.

Carbon dioxide is a major heat-trapping greenhouse gas. Its concentration in the atmosphere is now higher than at any time in at least the last 800,000 years. Although this is not new in the history of the planet, it is entirely new in human history. It is expected to have a negative impact on many ecosystems and humans across the world.

## Climate change isn't caused by human activity

Based on a huge amount of evidence, nearly all climate science experts are convinced that humans are affecting the climate by the way they live. The Met Office Hadley Centre is one of the world's leading centres for climate change research. It found that recent temperature rises and key changes in the Earth's environment could not be explained by natural climate change alone. Human activity is mainly responsible.

Scientific research and careful observation has shown that the concentration of greenhouse gases, which keep the Earth warm, is increasing. People are responsible for these increases by, for example, burning fossil fuels and cutting down forests.

## There's no scientific evidence for climate change

Scientists have been commenting on the relationship between emissions of gases and the climate since the 1800s. They have worked with governments to do something about climate change for a long time.

In 1988, the United Nations set up the Intergovernmental Panel on Climate Change (IPCC). The IPCC is a group of scientists from all parts of the world who assess the best available scientific and technical information on climate change.

The IPCC's 2007 Fourth Assessment Report warned of a rise in average global temperatures. This rise could be from 1.1 to 6.4 degrees Celsius above 1980-1999 levels by the end of this century, depending on future levels of emissions. Based on current research, the report said that recent temperature increases were very likely (over 90 per cent probable) to be the result of human activity.

## There's no point in me taking action

Every reduction in emissions makes a difference by not adding to the risk. Countries like the UK are in a position to set a positive example to the rest of the world. If the UK can rise to the challenge successfully, others will follow.

# Myths about climate change

## It's too late to make a difference

The last report from the IPCC in 2007 said that, if the world is to avoid dangerous climate change, global greenhouse gas emissions must:

▶ peak within the next decade or two;
▶ decline rapidly to well below current levels by the middle of the century.

This is still possible, and may be achieved with technologies that are available now. Putting off action to cut greenhouse gases will make it increasingly difficult and expensive to reduce emissions in the future. It will also create higher risks of severe climate change impacts.

*Based on a huge amount of evidence, nearly all climate science experts are convinced that humans are affecting the climate by the way they live.*

## It would cost too much to tackle climate change

Tackling climate change needn't damage the economy as a whole. Industry will have to adapt and jobs may change – but more may be created overall. Using less energy can also save companies and households money.

Not tackling climate change has a price too. The recent Stern report examines the economic impact of climate change. It estimates that not taking action could cost from five to 20 per cent of global GDP (gross domestic product) every year, now and forever. In comparison, reducing emissions to avoid the worst impacts of climate change could cost around one per cent of global GDP each year.

## Cutting my carbon footprint will affect my lifestyle

There are many small and simple things you can do that will contribute to big reductions in carbon emissions. Many actions will have little to no effect on your lifestyle – for example:

▶ turning off the lights when you leave a room;
▶ switching appliances off at the mains;
▶ turning your thermostat down one degree.

## Climate change will make life more comfortable in the UK

Climate change will lead to warmer winters, but temperatures will become uncomfortably hot in summer, and the climate may also be unpredictable and extreme. There's also the risk of rising sea levels and extreme weather like storms and floods. Tackling climate change and securing a more stable climate will make life a lot more comfortable.

*The above information is reprinted with kind permission from DirectGov. © Crown copyright*

**www.direct.gov.uk**

**Mini glossary**

**misconception** – a mistaken opinion

**carbon footprint** – a measure of an individual or company's effect on the environment, taking into account all greenhouse gas emissions for which they have been responsible

**GDP (Gross Domestic Product)** – an economic measure of a country's wealth; the total value of all goods and services produced by a country within a given time

# What about climate change in the future?

*WE SIMPLY DON'T KNOW EXACTLY what the UK's climate will do very long-term.*

How our climate will change depends on the future level of carbon dioxide and other gas emissions in the atmosphere. Some impacts are also highly unpredictable in a complex climatic system.

The experts believe there is no likelihood of the Gulf Stream closing down within the next two decades, but it is a possibility longer term.

So while we look set for a warmer – and stormier – climate for at least the next 20 to 30 years, very long-term who knows?

On the best projections now available from the International Climate Change Panel and UK Climate Impacts Programme, these are some of the anticipated changes over 75 years:

## Temperature

▶ Globally temperatures could rise anywhere between 1.5 and 5.8°C by 2080 – between two and eight times the rise we have already seen since 1900.

▶ Each degree of warming causes a lengthening of the growing season in the UK by between 1.5 weeks in the north and three weeks in the south.

▶ In the UK, an average temperature rise of 2-3.5°C is anticipated by 2080; though some areas could warm by nearly 6°C.

▶ More heat waves in summer are predicted – perhaps what we would now call an exceptional summer, like 1995, occurring two years out of three by 2080.

## Rain and snow

▶ Winters will become wetter (20-35 per cent wetter by 2080) and summers may become drier (35-50 per cent drier by 2080).

▶ Snowfalls will become increasingly rare – maybe up to 90 per cent less snow by 2080.

▶ Heavier rainfall events will become more frequent; though this cannot be quantified.

▶ Up to 50 per cent reduction in soil moisture content in south and east by 2080.

## The sea

(This is heavily dependent on the speed at which the Polar ice caps melt.)

▶ Extreme sea levels could occur between ten and 20 times more frequently by the 2080s.

▶ Relative sea level will continue to rise around most of the UK, perhaps by as much as 86 cm in south-east England.

▶ Sea temperatures are expected to continue to rise over the next couple of decades, though more slowly than the land temperature rises.

▶ The ranges shown here reflect the fact that we don't know future levels of carbon emissions which then determine climate.

**www.nationaltrust.org.uk**

## Mini glossary

*Gulf Stream* – a very powerful, warm ocean current which has an effect on the climate

*quantified* – to define or measure something with a numerical value

# Ten facts on climate science

**CLIMATE CHANGE IS HAPPENING, and it's because of us. Here are ten facts you should know.**

## 1 People say the world isn't really getting warmer, some years are just hotter than others, and it varies/goes around in cycles

The first decade of this century has been, by far, the warmest decade on the instrumental record. Despite 1998 being the warmest individual year, the last ten years have clearly been the warmest period in the 160-year record of global surface temperature.

Over the last 100 years the Earth has warmed by about 0.75 degrees Celsius and the speed at which it is warming is getting faster. These days the UK Spring arrives about ten days earlier than it did in the 1970s. In 160 years of records, the ten hottest years have been in the last 13 years.

Arctic sea ice is melting. The smallest amounts of Arctic summer ice on record were in the last three years: 2007-2009. In a few decades, large parts of the Arctic Ocean are expected to have no late summer sea-ice at all.

## 2 People say we've nothing to do with it

Carbon dioxide ($CO_2$) levels in the atmosphere have gone up 38%, to 387 parts per million, since pre-industrial times. Rising levels of greenhouse gases are directly linked to human activity, such as burning fossil fuels and clearing forests. There is a clear link between more greenhouse gases in the atmosphere and global warming.

## 3 But not all scientists agree though, right?

The overwhelming majority of climate scientists agree that human-induced climate change is a huge threat to the world. The Intergovernmental Panel on Climate Change is not run by any government – 'intergovernmental' means that it is made up of many different governments; 192 governments are currently signed up to it. Its reports are written by independent scientists and it is one of the most rigorous scientific bodies that exists. It brings together many thousands of scientists from countries all over the world to put together the best assessments of climate science available.

> **Scientists think that around 20% of species will become extinct with two degrees of warming.**

## 4 It's too late, we just need to accept it

The scientific consensus says we need to stop the world getting more than two degrees warmer than pre-industrial times if we want to avoid dangerous climate change. After that, in many regions, it will become harder to produce food, and competition for water, rises in sea level and loss of species will get much worse. We've got the technologies we need for a low-carbon world: we just need to go for it now. It'll cost much less to go low-carbon than it will to let climate change happen.

# Ten facts on climate science

## 5 A bit of melting ice and slightly hotter summers, what's the problem?

Global sea levels have already risen by about 17 centimetres since 1900, thanks to melting ice and warming oceans. This is already threatening low-lying countries, such as islands and Bangladesh. Millions more people are expected to be flooded every year by 2080. The global sea level could rise by up to 59 centimetres this century. In Europe alone this could affect over 20 million people. And it looks like the sea is rising more quickly now than in the 20th century.

## 6 Some countries have always had droughts, it's nothing new

Severe droughts are now twice as common as they were in 1970. More drought is affecting which crops we can grow effectively. Global demand for food is expected to nearly double by 2050, but lack of water could mean the world produces less food, not more.

## 7 Global warming is just to do with natural changes in the Sun

Scientists are clear: there is strong evidence that natural changes in solar radiation could not have caused the rapid warming we have seen over the past 50 years. Since the Industrial Revolution, additional greenhouse gases have had about ten times the effect on the climate forcing as changes in the Sun's output.

## 8 We've all got a lot on our plate – let's worry about it later

Even if all greenhouse gas emissions stopped tomorrow, we are already locked into a global temperature rise of at least 1.4°C (since 1750) because of the delayed impact between emissions and temperature change. It is already happening, and we need to act now to stop it getting much worse.

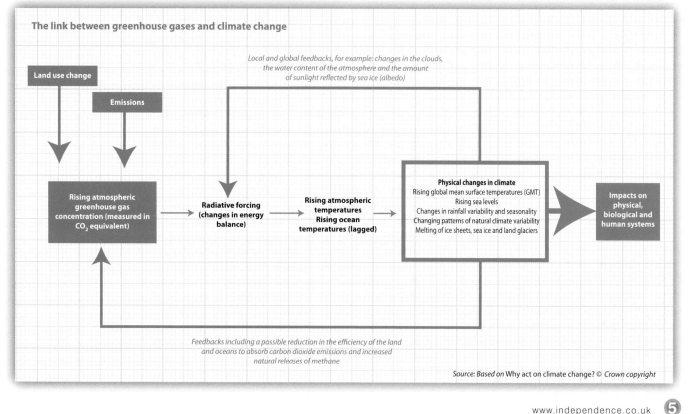

**The link between greenhouse gases and climate change**

Land use change

Emissions

*Local and global feedbacks, for example: changes in the clouds, the water content of the atmosphere and the amount of sunlight reflected by sea ice (albedo)*

Rising atmospheric greenhouse gas concentration (measured in $CO_2$ equivalent)

Radiative forcing (changes in energy balance)

Rising atmospheric temperatures
Rising ocean temperatures (lagged)

**Physical changes in climate**
Rising global mean surface temperatures (GMT)
Rising sea levels
Changes in rainfall variability and seasonality
Changing patterns of natural climate variability
Melting of ice sheets, sea ice and land glaciers

Impacts on physical, biological and human systems

*Feedbacks including a possible reduction in the efficiency of the land and oceans to absorb carbon dioxide emissions and increased natural releases of methane*

*Source: Based on* Why act on climate change? *© Crown copyright*

# Ten facts on climate science

> *Over the last 100 years the Earth has warmed by about 0.75 degrees Celsius and the speed at which it is warming is getting faster.*

**9**
## It won't happen to us though

Developed countries suffer impacts too. The 2003 heatwave in western Europe, which caused 35,000 deaths (2,000 in the UK), is already twice as likely to happen again next year. By the 2040s Europe will consider such a summer normal. By the 2060s they will consider it cool.

**10**
## Surely it's only the odd polar bear, who cares?

Species are already being forced to migrate or adapt. Scientists think that around 20% of species will become extinct with two degrees of warming – and it will be a real challenge, even if we act right now, to keep to that limit.

### Mini glossary

***human-induced*** – caused by humans

***rigorous*** – severe; accurate

***consensus*** – general agreement; the opinion of the majority

> *Even if all greenhouse gas emissions stopped tomorrow, we are already locked into a global temperature rise of at least 1.4°C.*

**www.decc.gov.uk**

I always thought we'd end up back here... but not quite so soon!

# The social and economic impacts of climate change

*INFORMATION FROM Earthwatch.*

## Social impacts

Climate change is likely to have far-reaching and catastrophic social impacts and will affect communities in different ways. Vulnerability to climate change impacts depends on differences in geography, technological resources, governance and wealth. It is often the world's poorest nations that are most vulnerable to the effects of climate change – nations that have the fewest resources to adapt and cope with these effects. Communities in developing countries which are making little or no direct contribution to climate change are likely to be among the most affected.

> **Changing climates and weather patterns will alter the amount of tourism to certain countries, since the appeal of tourism relies heavily on the natural environment.**

## Water shortages

Declining rainfall and increased evaporation may reduce run-off, threatening the availability of fresh water for human and industrial consumption. Furthermore, loss of glaciers and ice fields may jeopardise drinking water supplies. Water supply is likely to be affected both in terms of quantity and in quality as demand for reduced supplies increases. Loss of water (and food) security may lead to increased conflict. In Kenya, for example, there have been territorial disputes over receding bodies of water, and increases in cattle raiding and violence, as people who have historically managed through periods of drought and food shortages find themselves dealing with unprecedented famine.

## Food shortages

Climate change will affect food production, as well as how much food is available to people (food security). Increases in temperature in high latitudes will extend the growing range of some agricultural crops, changing seasons will affect the growing seasons, and increased atmospheric $CO_2$ will boost agricultural productivity.

These potential benefits, however, will be matched by altered weather patterns which will increase crop vulnerabilities to infection, pest infestations and choking weeds. This will not only decrease yields of crops, but also force farmers to increase their use of harmful and expensive pesticides and herbicides. The increase in extreme weather events will affect both developed and developing countries, although developed countries have more resources to deal with vulnerabilities.

If climate change is not avoided, an additional 80 to 120 million people will be at risk of hunger. 70 to 80% of these people will be in Africa, and the majority are likely to be women, who have a greater reliance on subsistence farming.

## Health

The health implications of climate change are profound. Climate change will increase experience of heat stress, injury and death from natural disasters (such as floods and windstorms), vector-borne diseases (such as malaria, dengue, schistosomiasis and tick-borne diseases), water- and food-borne diseases. The elderly and women are likely to be disproportionately affected by the increased disease burden. In developing countries like Africa, where severe health problems such as malaria, HIV/AIDS and hunger-related diseases are already widespread, the added health implications of climate change are likely to result in an increase in human death rates.

# The social and economic impacts of climate change

## Economic impacts

### Agricultural production

Changes in climate will impact on agriculture and food production in many ways. Production may increase with higher temperatures in middle and higher latitudes, since the length of the potential growing season may be increased. Crop-producing areas may expand towards the poles in countries such as Canada and Russia, and in some regions new opportunities will occur for growing new crops such as grapes for wine.

Increasing levels of $CO_2$ will impact on different crops in different ways, by affecting the rate of photosynthesis. Experiments have demonstrated that crops such as wheat, rice and soybeans respond positively to increased $CO_2$ by increased growth, whereas other crops such as sugarcane, millet and corn are less responsive.

Agriculture of any kind is strongly influenced by the availability of water. The demand for water for irrigation is projected to rise in a warmer climate. Falling water levels and the resulting increase in the energy needed to pump water will make the practice of irrigation more expensive, particularly when, with drier conditions, more water will be required.

Agricultural pests may increase in warmer climates. Longer growing seasons will enable insects such as grasshoppers to complete a greater number of reproductive cycles during the spring, summer and autumn. Warmer winter temperatures may also allow larvae to over-winter in areas where they are now limited by cold, thus causing greater infestation during the following crop season.

### Developing countries' economies and climate change

The economies of developing countries are highly dependent on agriculture and ecosystems, and changes in agricultural output will definitely affect these nations. 61% of people in South Asia and 64% in sub-Saharan Africa are employed in the rural agricultural sector, and the agricultural sector is the most at risk from climate change.

The economic strain of coping with the many social impacts of climate change on countries (and especially developing countries) such as reduced food security, increase of extreme weather events such as flooding and increased diseases such as malaria, will be great. For example, Zimbabwe suffered from an extreme drought from 1991 to 1992 which caused GDP (Gross Domestic Product) to fall by 9% and inflation to increase by 46%. Government spending on education and health was sacrificed for drought-related emergency outlays. An altered climate may mean that people or governments coping with its effects will be locked into a poverty trap as the majority of their income and assets are spent on coping strategies rather than profit-making strategies.

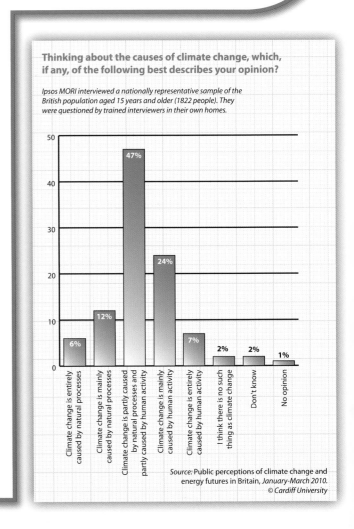

**Thinking about the causes of climate change, which, if any, of the following best describes your opinion?**

*Ipsos MORI interviewed a nationally representative sample of the British population aged 15 years and older (1822 people). They were questioned by trained interviewers in their own homes.*

- Climate change is entirely caused by natural processes: 6%
- Climate change is mainly caused by natural processes: 12%
- Climate change is partly caused by natural processes and partly caused by human activity: 47%
- Climate change is mainly caused by human activity: 24%
- Climate change is entirely caused by human activity: 7%
- I think there is no such thing as climate change: 2%
- Don't know: 2%
- No opinion: 1%

*Source:* Public perceptions of climate change and energy futures in Britain, *January-March 2010.*
© *Cardiff University*

# The social and economic impacts of climate change

*"Vulnerability to climate change impacts depends on differences in geography, technological resources, governance and wealth."*

## Tourism

Tourism is one of the fastest-growing industries in the European Union and the most important industry in many developing countries. Changing climates and weather patterns will alter the amount of tourism to certain countries, since the appeal of tourism relies heavily on the natural environment.

While tourism may become a victim of climate change, it also contributes to climate change through air travel. Air travel accounts for around 3% of $CO_2$ emissions and the International Panel on Climate Change expects this to increase to 7% by 2050.

Some destinations – such as the Maldives, which are vulnerable to sea-level rise – could see reduced numbers of tourists, while the Mediterranean will experience an increased number of extreme heat days (above 40°C) which could deter tourists. Winter tourism and the skiing industry are under threat due to shorter ski seasons and unpredictable snow conditions. In the European Alps, skiing represents about 5% of Alpine countries' GDP; therefore, the threat of loss of skiing and winter sports tourism could impact heavily on these countries' economies.

## Forestry

A report compiled by the Forestry Commission predicted that under various climate change forecasts, the growing distribution and productivity of different commercially-grown tree species will be altered. For example, Sitka Spruce will be unable to be grown at low altitudes, but will show increased productivity at higher altitudes in the UK, whereas future climates will decrease the range and productivity of Scot's Pine across the whole of the UK. In addition, an increase in the frequency of forest fires due to more droughts and less precipitation in some areas will affect the forestry industry.

*It is estimated that by 2050 there will be 250 million people who will be forced to flee their homes due to drought, desertification, sea-level rise and extreme weather events. These migrants are known as climate change refugees. Many human populations on islands in the Pacific have already become victims of climate change.*

*"Climate change will affect food production, as well as how much food is available to people."*

The above information is reprinted with kind permission from the Earthwatch Institute. © Earthwatch Institute

**www.earthwatch.org**

## Mini glossary

**catastrophic** – *destructive; terrible*

**run-off** – *rainwater which feeds streams and rivers*

**unprecedented** – *never previously known or experienced*

**profound** – *thorough; significant*

**disproportionately** – *not in proportion; excessively or extremely*

# Climate change: the forest connection

*MOST PEOPLE ARE NOW AWARE that the world's hunger for energy from fossil fuel is leading to catastrophic climate change. What is also becoming increasingly clear is the effect that forests have on the climate and the climate has on forests – and how changes in one system will affect the other.*

## Forests' effect on the climate

Forests play an important role in regulating the Earth's temperature and weather patterns by storing large quantities of carbon and water. This regulatory function has a significant effect on both the local and the global climate.

Locally, trees provide shade, which in turn lowers summer temperatures and prevents the soil from drying out. They reduce heat loss from the ground in winter and reduce storm damage by providing shelter from wind.

Globally, forests regulate the global carbon cycle, having a profound effect on the climate. As well as this, deforestation is also contributing to climate change. Indeed, the $CO_2$ released each year from forest loss is higher than that released by our yearly transport emissions. The continued existence of forests is particularly necessary if we are to stop what is known as runaway climate change. Runaway climate change is the point whereby increases in temperature lead to more greenhouse gas emissions which in turn leads to increased temperatures.

> *Global warming, on a geological timescale, is occurring in the equivalent of a split second.*

Apparently it's for a housing estate.

It used to be our housing estate!

> **DID YOU KNOW**
>
> *UN-REDD was launched in 2008 and aims to assist 36 developing countries to put in place strategies which reduce emissions from deforestation and forest degradation (REDD).*

> *Forests play an important role in regulating the Earth's temperature and weather patterns by storing large quantities of carbon and water.*

# Climate change: the forest connection

> *Efforts to tackle forest loss must not justify more fossil fuel emissions in other areas.*

## The climate's effect on forests

Global warming, on a geological timescale, is occurring in the equivalent of a split second. It is significantly disrupting the complex and poorly-understood interactions associated with forest ecosystems. This means that in around a third of today's forests the species of trees will change. A temperature increase of 3°C by 2100 would result in forest ecosystems having to 'move' 500km towards the poles or 500 metres higher in order to find the same climatic conditions. Such distances are far beyond the average rate of distribution for individual tree species, let alone entire forest ecosystems.

According to the Intergovernmental Panel on Climate Change (IPCC), a United Nations panel of climate scientists, it is likely that many tree species will not be able to change their geographic distribution fast enough to keep up with expected shifts in suitable climate. Because of this, increased rates of extinctions are expected to occur.

## What can be done?

So forests (or the lack of them) are one of the key problems that must be tackled if we are to minimise the effects of climate change. It is not surprising then that many have also suggested planting trees (sometimes called carbon sinks) or reducing emissions from deforestation and degradation (REDD) are among the solutions to our climate crisis.

SinksWatch believes, however, that while urgent action is needed to stop forest loss and restore degraded forests, both of these solutions – REDD and carbon sinks – are not the best way to tackle climate change. REDD and carbon sinks are concepts that are linked to a global carbon market. This means that planting trees or reducing deforestation in one place (usually the global South) can be used to justify even more fossil fuel emissions somewhere else (usually in an industrialised country). And many of these carbon sink projects have financed the expansion of large-scale industrial tree plantations. SinksWatch believes that efforts to tackle forest loss must not justify more fossil fuel emissions in other areas, because such a trade-off would neither help stop runaway climate change nor help save forests in the long run. Runaway climate change will also have a major negative impact on the world's forests.

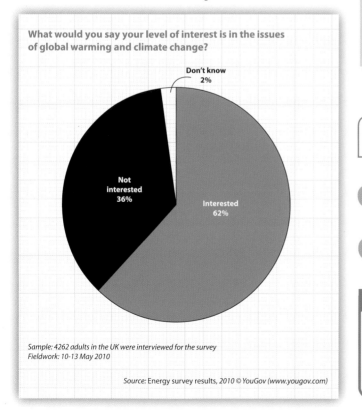

**What would you say your level of interest is in the issues of global warming and climate change?**

- Don't know 2%
- Not interested 36%
- Interested 62%

*Sample: 4262 adults in the UK were interviewed for the survey*
*Fieldwork: 10-13 May 2010*

*Source: Energy survey results, 2010 © YouGov (www.yougov.com)*

The above information is reprinted with kind permission from SinksWatch. © SinksWatch

**www.sinkswatch.org**

**www.fern.org**

### Mini glossary

***degradation*** *– the breakdown of a structure or function; in the context of a forest ecosystem, degradation can lead to a loss in production and biodiversity*

# Climate change scepticism

**A SUMMARY OF A SURVEY carried out by YouGov.**

*By Zara Atkinson*

The British public is becoming less, not more, concerned about climate change, a survey for the energy company EDF has found. Considering the structure of the new Conservative-Liberal Democrat Coalition Government, it is interesting to note a significant difference in the views of the two parties' supporters on these issues. Liberal Democrat supporters are the most likely to be interested in global warming and climate change, at 79%, compared to 53% of Conservative supporters.

> ❝ *Nuclear power, hailed by some as a green power alternative, appears to be gaining support as a source for Britain's future energy.* ❞

The survey results indicate that concern for global warming and climate change is continuing to decrease. Although 28% of the public agreed with the statement that 'it is a serious and urgent problem and radical steps must be taken NOW to prevent terrible damage being done to the planet', this is down from 38% who agreed in 2007; a 10% drop in three years. Again, far more Liberal Democrat supporters think this way (43%) than supporters of the Conservatives (18%).

> ❝ *Liberal Democrat supporters are the most likely to be interested in global warming and climate change, at 79%, compared to 53% of Conservative supporters.* ❞

## 'Not clear whether climate change is happening or not'

After the University of East Anglia's Climatic Research Unit leaked documents which suggested that data not supporting global warming theories were deliberately being withheld, it is perhaps not surprising that more of the public are becoming sceptical about the existence of climate change.

One-third (33%) of the public now agrees with the statement 'it is not yet clear whether climate change is happening or not – scientists are divided on this issue', compared to only 25% in 2007.

There also seem to be many more sceptics among Conservative supporters, 43% of whom agreed with the statement.

Only 20% of Liberal Democrat supporters thought the same.

Nuclear power, hailed by some as a green power alternative, appears to be gaining support as a source for Britain's future energy. As most of Britain's older nuclear and coal power stations will come to the end of their useful lives by about 2020, a substantial 'power gap' will need to be filled. 52% of Britons now support the gap being filled by new nuclear power stations (up 6% from 46% in 2007), while 64% agree with the statement 'nuclear energy has disadvantages but the country needs it as part of the energy balance, with coal, gas and wind power' (an increase of 5% from 59% in 2007). Just 18% now agree that 'the most important thing is to stop building nuclear power stations' compared to 24% in 2007. And while the source of power may be in dispute, the need for Britain to be self-sufficient in energy seems certain: 90% now agree with this, exactly the same as did in 2007.

*27 May 2010*

**www.yougov.com**

# Climate change blame?

*SUMMARY OF A YouGov survey.*

A significant 84% of people agreed with the statement that the planet is warming.

18% believe human activity is mainly responsible.

The majority of the British public believe that Planet Earth is experiencing climate change, but few place the blame entirely on human activity.

Most people (58%) feel that other factors have a part to play.

8% think that human activity, in comparison to other factors, is not responsible at all.

A small but noticeable 8% refute the idea that the planet is warming at all.

It seems that most Britons also believe that politicians are not doing enough to tackle global warming with 73% agreeing with the statement that 'there is no serious political will worldwide to tackle climate change'. This is perhaps due to the results of the Copenhagen summit, which was a major disappointment due to its failure to reach consensus between the participating nations.

It seems that the recent 'climategate' controversy surrounding scientific evidence to support the extent, and causes of, the warming has created a huge amount of uncertainty around the issue. In fact, 30% of the public claim that they have become more sceptical about the validity of climate change and 38% agree that dishonest scientists have made them doubt whether climate change is really happening.

*9 April 2010*

 **DID YOU KNOW?** *The Copenhagen summit was a climate change conference which took place in 2009. However, politicians at the summit failed to reach any concrete conclusions and no legally binding commitments were made.*

*The above information is reprinted with kind permission from YouGov.*
*© YouGov*

**www.yougov.com**

 *Most Britons also believe that politicians are not doing enough to tackle global warming.*

## Mini glossary

**sceptical** – *doubtful; prone to disbelief*

# Activities

## Brainstorm

Brainstorm to find out what you know about the science behind climate change.

1.  What do you know about the main causes of climate change? Try to find examples of natural and human causes of climate change.

    .......................................................................................................................................................

    .......................................................................................................................................................

2.  List three major global effects of climate change.

    .......................................................................................................................................................

    .......................................................................................................................................................

## Oral activities

3.  Role play a radio chat show on the topic of climate change. One member of the group should play the show's host, a second should play a climate change expert and a third a climate change sceptic. Try to get a lively debate going. Other students can play listeners phoning in with questions for the panel. The host should aim to give equal time to both sides of the argument.

    NOTES...............................................................................................................................................

    .......................................................................................................................................................

    .......................................................................................................................................................

4.  Give a brief presentation on the effects of climate change. You should aim to speak for about five minutes on the global effects of climate change, and a further five minutes on how climate change may affect your country and region locally. You can use Powerpoint to help you if you wish. You should answer questions from other students at the end of your presentation.

    NOTES...............................................................................................................................................

    .......................................................................................................................................................

    .......................................................................................................................................................

## Moral dilemma

5.  You would like to go abroad for your summer holiday next year and have been looking forward to it for a long time. However, you know the emissions from air travel are a major contributor to global warming. Do you travel by air anyway, or look at alternatives which would be better for the planet?

# Activities

## Research activities

6.  Read two newspapers, one broadsheet and one tabloid, over a week. Cut out any articles which refer to climate change or global warming. When you have collected all your articles, read and review them. Do you think climate change receives enough press coverage? Do the articles mostly support the idea of human-induced climate change or reject it?

    CONCLUSION ..........................................................................................................................................................................

    ................................................................................................................................................................................................

    ................................................................................................................................................................................................

7.  The article *The social and economic impacts of climate change* on pages 7-9, refers to food shortages. Using the Internet, carry out your own research into how climate change will affect the world's food supply. Which types of food will be most affected? Write a summary of your findings.

    NOTES .....................................................................................................................................................................................

    ................................................................................................................................................................................................

    ................................................................................................................................................................................................

## Written activities

Complete the following activities in your exercise books or on a sheet of paper.

8.  Imagine you are a climate refugee. You have had to leave your island home because of rising sea levels and frequent flooding. Write a diary entry exploring your experiences and emotions. What effect do you think it would have on your life? How would you learn to adapt to your new home? Do you think you would be more conscious of human impact on the global climate if it meant you had to move away from your home?

9.  Write an article for your school newspaper about the effect of the world's forests on our climate. You can use *Climate change: the forest connection* on pages 10-11 to help you. Explain the relationship between forests and the climate in an engaging and informative way.

## Design activities

10. Design an A2 illustrated wall poster outlining the causes and effects of global climate change.

11. Read *Climate change blame?* on page 13. Choose two of the statistics provided and create a set of graphs to display them clearly. You will need to choose what type of graph would be best suited to the information given. Remember to title your graphs.

# Adapting to the greenhouse

**INFORMATION FROM Panos London.**

> *Poor people are highly vulnerable because they have little hope of earning a decent living or finding a safe place to live.*

## The response to climate change – what can be done?

Climate change is a global issue and needs a global response – whether creating mitigation and adaptation strategies, providing funding for these strategies, or through additional policy assistance for people who are especially vulnerable to climate change.

## Mitigation and adaptation

- Mitigation needs international agreement and national enforcement; emissions from one country threaten everybody, and cutting them will take time. Adaptation, on the other hand, is immediate and local: people who are affected by climate change make the changes, pay the costs and feel the benefits.

- A global response to climate change needs to include both mitigation and adaptation, and have input from many quarters. For example, researchers could work on developing existing adaptation techniques or finding new ways to adapt (other than drastic options such as migration); journalists could then inform people of the existing options and costs.

- Communities must also come together to make their voices stronger at international policy forums.

- Countries and communities must find new ways to manage their resources – for example, by planting climate-suitable crops that tolerate or resist drought, salt and pests. Governments also need to improve planning regulations and bring in fresh policies to encourage low-energy buildings and transport systems and the use of recycled water.

- Existing communication networks could play a vital role in this process. Governments can become more prepared for disasters by providing early warning of epidemics and natural disasters. The media could play a vital part in broadcasting information rapidly and to a large number of people. It is also important to make use of local knowledge systems, and for communities to share knowledge between themselves (for example, farmer to farmer). For example, a Practical Action project in Zimbabwe found that radio was the most efficient mode of communication.

> *Climate change is a global issue and needs a global response.*

We're away from rising sea levels and close to our food sources!

# Adapting to the greenhouse

## Reducing vulnerability

Poor people are highly vulnerable because they have little hope of earning a decent living or finding a safe place to live. Women in subsistence farming communities are particularly vulnerable. Their lack of access to, and rights over, resources and wealth such as agricultural land, combined with fragile property rights, leave them more exposed in a changing climate. They are often more vulnerable than men to weather-related disasters, partly because they bear a greater burden of care for their families.

Changing policies away from reacting to disasters, to more proactive capacity building can reduce gender inequality. Higher incomes, better education and technical skills, better food distribution, disaster preparedness and management and improved healthcare can all substantially reduce climate vulnerability.

Adaptation is sustainable when it is linked to effective governance, civil and political rights, and literacy – in other words, when it is part of mainstream national development planning. Not enough information and knowledge about climate change will continue to prevent effective adaptation. More relevant information is therefore vital – for example about increased crop yields linked to changes in planting dates, or the cost of coastal protection investment. But Asia and Africa face other urgent priorities, such as domestic conflicts, widespread poverty, hunger, epidemics and terrorism. In these situations, it is easy for people to forget about climate change and the need to adapt.

**DID YOU KNOW?** Development of the tourism industry will be affected by climate change, as mangroves, coral reefs and fisheries suffer. For example, following a 30 per cent loss of corals in 1997/98, tourism fell in Mombasa and Zanzibar, with estimated financial losses of US$12–18 million.

> " Adaptation is sustainable when it is linked to effective governance, civil and political rights, and literacy. "

The above information is reprinted with kind permission from Panos London. © Panos London

**www.panos.org.uk**

## Mini glossary

**epidemics** – widespread outbreaks of diseases amongst a population

**subsistence farming** – farming only enough produce to support your own family with none left over to sell

**capacity building** – increasing poor and vulnerable communities' skills, knowledge and capabilities in order to enhance development

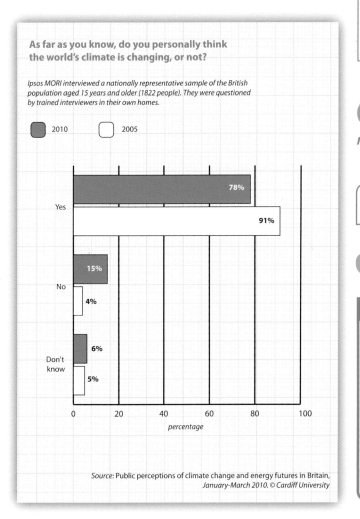

**As far as you know, do you personally think the world's climate is changing, or not?**

*Ipsos MORI interviewed a nationally representative sample of the British population aged 15 years and older (1822 people). They were questioned by trained interviewers in their own homes.*

■ 2010    □ 2005

Yes: 78% (2010), 91% (2005)
No: 15% (2010), 4% (2005)
Don't know: 6% (2010), 5% (2005)

percentage (0–100)

*Source: Public perceptions of climate change and energy futures in Britain, January-March 2010. © Cardiff University*

# The Kyoto Protocol

**INFORMATION FROM** *Learning and Teaching Scotland.*

The Kyoto Protocol was the world's first international agreement on how to tackle climate change, and an important tool that governments around the world have used since it was made law in 2005. By 2009, 183 countries had signed up to the Protocol and had made a commitment to reduce their carbon dioxide emissions and five other greenhouse gases by an average of 5.2%.

Many countries set their own targets. In the EU this was originally 8% but later increased to 20% by 2020, as governments began to realise that much more had to be done. In the UK and Scotland, climate bills more recently committed to reductions of 80%.

## Stopping dangerous climate change

The main aim of the Kyoto Protocol was to hold greenhouse gases at a level that will stop dangerous changes to the planet's climate system. All of the industrialised nations that signed and ratified the Protocol would collectively reduce their emissions.

*Most people agree that the Kyoto Protocol has been an important step towards recognising and tackling the problem of climate change.*

## Common problem but different responsibilities

The Kyoto Protocol recognised that we have a common problem but that not all countries have contributed to this problem in the same way. Some countries, including China and India, were exempted from targets because they were not main contributors during the period of industrialisation that is believed to be the cause of climate change.

## Criticism

The United States and Australia originally opted out of Kyoto because of the exemptions granted to China, India and developing countries. They also claimed, along with some economists, that it would cost jobs and damage their countries' economies. However, Australia later signed Kyoto after a change of leadership in 2007, and the US has recently begun working towards its own climate bill.

Many people criticised Kyoto because its rules created a carbon marketplace, where carbon credits could be traded. This allowed richer nations to avoid cutting their emissions and, in some cases, disguise an increase.

Another major criticism was that the original targets of 5.2% would make little impact on the main cause of climate change – human-induced emissions.

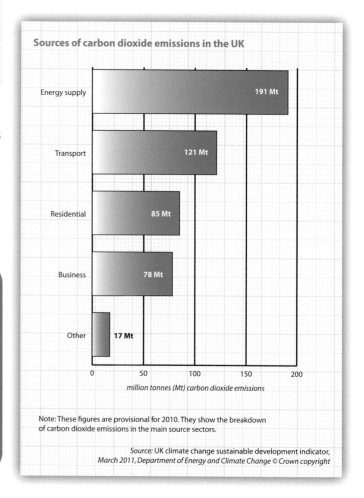

**Sources of carbon dioxide emissions in the UK**

| Sector | Emissions |
|---|---|
| Energy supply | 191 Mt |
| Transport | 121 Mt |
| Residential | 85 Mt |
| Business | 78 Mt |
| Other | 17 Mt |

*million tonnes (Mt) carbon dioxide emissions*

Note: These figures are provisional for 2010. They show the breakdown of carbon dioxide emissions in the main source sectors.

*Source: UK climate change sustainable development indicator, March 2011, Department of Energy and Climate Change © Crown copyright*

# The Kyoto Protocol

## Has the Kyoto Protocol stopped dangerous climate change?

The first phase of Kyoto is due to expire in 2012. It has had its successes and difficulties, and many countries' emissions have actually increased since ratifying the Kyoto Protocol. Many other countries (such as most European countries, the UK and Scotland) have, however, succeeded in reducing their emissions. Most people agree that the Kyoto Protocol has been an important step towards recognising and tackling the problem of climate change. It put climate change on the worldwide agenda for governments.

Most people also agree that not enough has been done to avoid dangerous climate change and that the original Kyoto targets were not strict enough. Since the first Kyoto, climate science has become more alarming and predictions of warming have become more severe. It is now widely held that temperatures are rising and, to prevent the climate from becoming dangerously unstable, emissions will need to be reduced by at least 80% around the world as quickly as possible.

WE SEEM TO HAVE STRUCK SOME SORT OF BARRIER?

*The above information is reprinted with kind permission from Learning and Teaching Scotland. © Crown copyright, 2011*

www.ltscotland.org.uk/ exploringclimatechange/response/ kyotoprotocol.asp

**Mini glossary**

*ratified* – made a contract legally binding

# Carbon offsets

INFORMATION FROM THE David Suzuki Foundation.

## What is a carbon offset?

A carbon offset is a credit for greenhouse gas reductions achieved by one party that can be purchased and used to compensate (offset) the emissions of another party. Carbon offsets are typically measured in tonnes of $CO_2$-equivalents (or $CO_2e$) and are bought and sold through a number of international brokers, online retailers and trading platforms.

For example, wind energy companies often sell carbon offsets. The wind energy company benefits because the carbon offsets it sells make such projects more economically viable. The buyers of the offsets benefit because they can claim that their purchase resulted in new non-polluting energy, which they can use to offset their own greenhouse gas emissions. The buyers may also save money as it may be less expensive for them to purchase offsets than to eliminate their own emissions.

Many types of activities can generate carbon offsets. Renewable energy such as the wind farm example above, or installations of solar, small hydro, geothermal and biomass energy can all create carbon offsets by displacing fossil fuels. Other types of offsets available for sale on the market include those resulting from energy-efficiency projects, for example methane capture from landfills or livestock, reforestation or the destruction of powerful greenhouse gases.

> A carbon offset is a credit for greenhouse gas reductions achieved by one party that can be purchased and used to compensate (offset) the emissions of another party.

## The Gold Standard for carbon offsets

The Gold Standard is widely considered to be the highest standard in the world for carbon offsets. It ensures that key environmental criteria have been met by offset projects that carry its label. Significantly, only offsets from energy efficiency and renewable-energy projects qualify for the Gold Standard, as these projects encourage a shift away from fossil-fuel use and carry very low environmental risks. Tree-planting projects are explicitly excluded by The Gold Standard.

**Index ranking of the ten largest carbon dioxide emitters**

| Country | Share of global $CO_2$ emissions | CCPI rank 2011 | CCPI rank 2012 |
|---|---|---|---|
| United Kingdom | 1.61% | 8 | 5 |
| Germany | 2.59% | 7 | 6 |
| India | 5.47% | 10 | 23 |
| Korea, Rep. | 1.78% | 34 | 41 |
| Japan | 3.77% | 38 | 43 |
| United States | 17.91% | 54 | 52 |
| Canada | 1.80% | 57 | 54 |
| Russian Federation | 5.28% | 48 | 55 |
| China | 23.71% | 56 | 57 |
| Iran | 1.84% | 52 | 60 |

Note: The Climate Change Performance Index (CCPI) evaluates the climate protection performance of 57 different countries responsible for more than 90% of global carbon dioxide emissions. The lower the ranking, the lower the country's climate protection performance. Visit http://www.germanwatch.org/klima/ccpi.htm for more information.

*Source:* The climate change performance index, 2011 © Germanwatch

# Carbon offsets

## Why some carbon offsets are better than others

As with any purchase, buyers need to choose their offsets carefully, particularly as the voluntary offset market is largely unregulated.

One issue to consider is the offset project type. For example, although quite popular, offsets from tree-planting projects are problematic for a number of reasons, including their lack of permanence and the fact that these projects do not alter our dependence on fossil fuels.

Offset projects involving the destruction of powerful greenhouse gases, such as halocarbon gases, have also been heavily criticised. Due to the sheer volume of offsets and profits that they generate, and the low price of purchasing them, they actually create an incentive for more ozone-depleting gases to be created, in order to make a profit from buying an offset. They also tend to flood the market and squeeze out more sustainable offset projects, like solar and wind.

Other criteria of high-quality carbon offsets include: validation of the project by respectable third-parties; steps by the project developer to ensure that each offset is only sold once (e.g. by listing the offsets on a public registry); and systems in place to control 'leakage', where the creation of a GHG reduction in one region causes an unintended increase in GHG emissions somewhere else (e.g. protecting a forest in one location could simply shift logging to a forested area in a new location).

*errr... I'm just on my way to plant some trees to offset my emmissions!*

The above information is reprinted with kind permission from the David Suzuki Foundation. © David Suzuki Foundation

**www.davidsuzuki.org**

## Mini glossary

*viable* – feasible; achievable

*validation* – approval; acceptance

# Key agreements in the history of climate change

TIMELINE OF THE MOST IMPORTANT agreements throughout recent history.

By Amy Himsworth

## November 1988 – Formation of the Intergovernmental Panel on Climate Change

The Intergovernmental Panel on Climate Change (IPCC) was formed, made up of leading scientists and climate change experts. It held its first meeting in Geneva and aims to assess scientific knowledge on climate change, analyse its effects and formulate practical solutions.

*A disappointing result was achieved at the Copenhagen conference when a weak deal was reached between the US, Brazil, India, South Africa and China.*

## August 1990 – Publication of IPCC's First Assessment Report

The IPCC's First Assessment Report concluded that man-made emissions were adding to the natural greenhouse gases in the atmosphere. Unless measures were adopted to limit emissions, this addition would lead to an average increase in global temperature.

## June 1992 – Signing of the United Nations Framework Convention on Climate Change

At the Rio Earth Summit, the United Nations Framework Convention on Climate Change (UNFCCC) was signed by 154 countries. The main objective was to stabilise greenhouse gases in the atmosphere 'at a level that would prevent dangerous interference with the climate system'.

## December 1997 – Signing of the Kyoto Protocol

More than 150 countries signed the Kyoto Protocol, which bound 38 developed countries to reduce greenhouse gas emissions by at least 5% below 1990 levels for the years 2008-2012. Developing nations, including China, had no formal binding targets.

## December 2001 – Rules on implementation of the Kyoto Protocol finalised

The final, detailed rules for the implementation of the Kyoto Protocol were agreed. Australia, the US, Japan and Canada forced the European Union to accept major concessions so that a final agreement could be reached.

# Key agreements in the history of climate change

## December 2010 – UN climate change conference in Cancún

Elements agreed by the UN in Cancún included: a Green Climate Fund, which would transfer money from the developed to the developing world to tackle the impacts of climate change; the arrangement of money and technology for developing countries to build their own sustainable futures.

## February 2005 – The Kyoto Protocol becomes law

**The Kyoto Protocol became international law.**

> The IPCC's First Assessment Report (1990) concluded that man-made emissions were adding to the natural greenhouse gases in the atmosphere.

## April 2011 – UN climate change negotiations in Bangkok

UNFCCC Executive Secretary Christiana Figueres called on governments to tackle work settled in the 2010 Cancún talks and address shortfalls in climate action. Detailed discussions were held on how to put into practice certain aspects, such as the creation of new technology for developing countries.

## July 2009 – G8 countries reach agreement

The G8 countries (US, UK, France, Germany, Italy, Canada, Japan and Russia) decided that a limit of two degrees of average global warming should not be exceeded. In order to reach this goal, global greenhouse gas emissions should be cut by at least 50% by 2050.

## December 2009 – UN climate summit in Copenhagen

A disappointing result was achieved at the Copenhagen conference when a weak deal was reached between the US, Brazil, India, South Africa and China. The agreement 'recognised' the importance of limiting the global temperature rise to two degrees, but no legally binding commitments were required.

> A disappointing result was achieved at the 2009 Copenhagen conference when a weak deal was reached between the US, Brazil, India, South Africa and China.

May 2011

# We have to adapt culturally to climate change

*AN ARTICLE BY DR JENNY PICKERILL, Senior Lecturer in Human Geography, University of Leicester.*

While the case that climate change is happening and is probably irreversible is strong, the political arguments about whether we should do anything about it remain ongoing and unresolved. Many in the minority world (like Britain and the USA) are relying upon technological innovation (like wind power, electric cars and geo-engineering) to save us. Research shows that while many individuals have engaged in making small changes in their lifestyle – such as using recycling bins or cycling a little more – most struggle to make big behavioural changes and feel powerless to take on the changes necessary to really stop further carbon emissions. Time is running out to make changes at a big enough scale to mitigate further climatic changes.

> **Adapting to climate change is necessary but complex.**

> **We need to be designing houses which will be suitable for the future climate of wet, hot, unpredictable weather.**

For a start, climate change is likely to lead to more extreme climatic events; an unpredictability that is difficult to plan for. Predicting what climatic changes will occur is a difficult science, let alone interpreting what that means for how we live. Moreover, the size of climate changes depends on whether we can reduce carbon emissions now, keep them stable, or increase them yet further. So if we are to take the adaptation route, we have to plan for a variety of different scenarios and we should not abandon all attempts at mitigation. Mitigation has effectively become about trying to reduce the extent to which we need to adapt: it is not an either/or situation.

Adapting is sometimes suggested as the easier option. Rather than fundamentally changing everything about how we live today, we could plan for a different future and increase our resilience to any changes ahead. There is, of course, just as much debate as to how we should prepare for these changes as there is about how to mitigate climate change. We should be careful not to be naive about what this actually involves.

> **Time is running out to make changes at a big enough scale to mitigate further climatic changes.**

# We have to adapt culturally to climate change

## Housing

If we take housing as an example, we can begin to understand the complexity and possibility of making these changes. Housing – both in construction and use – consumes significant amounts of energy and contributes at least 25% of all carbon emissions in Britain. The Met Office predict that temperatures will rise in Britain, with increasing heatwaves and fewer frost days. At the same time we will have increased rainfall, more intensive rain showers, sea-level rise, coastal surge events and more storms. In other words, we need to be prepared for flooding, storms and heat. If we don't, then not only will our houses suffer from damage but we will continue to increase our use of energy as more people need air conditioning to keep their houses cool – creating a vicious circle of increased emissions and then greater temperature rises.

We are building eco-housing that is suitable for today's climate and reduces carbon emissions (mitigating climate change), both of which are important, but it is not enough. We need to be designing houses which will be suitable for the future climate of wet, hot, unpredictable weather.

In practical terms this raises questions about whether we should be designing our houses to be more temporary or more durable, training more of us to be able to build our own houses and use more easily available local materials (like we did in the past before the development of bricks). It is also about all of us understanding the subtle balance between the need for insulation and ventilation. We need insulation to reduce draughts and keep us warm but we need ventilation to keep us cool. As the climate changes we are likely to need more ventilation than insulation, which could dramatically change the design of our houses.

As soon as we start to talk of building better houses the issue of our existing housing stock is raised. Of course we need to improve these too, but so far we have focused on quite small changes (such as extra insulation) or adding technology to houses. We need to think more radically about how to adapt these houses to survive climate change, not just reduce carbon emissions.

Finally, adapting housing for climate change involves considerably more than technical changes to construction; it involves huge cultural shifts in how we consider our house and home. For many, a house is first and foremost about security – both the physical aspect of having somewhere safe to live and sleep, and financially as an investment – and comfort. There is a deeply-felt sense that our homes are our refuge. To change this, by making housing more temporary, using natural materials (which might be perceived as less robust), or relying on manual heating and ventilation systems, requires social changes in how we live.

Moreover, it requires us to build ready for changes that many of us have only vaguely understood to be happening; to change behaviour for an unknown future. It is not technology, or really even politics, which is holding us back in making these changes, it is deep-rooted cultural and social understandings of how we live and what we expect houses to do for us.

As a result, we can understand adapting to climate change is necessary but complex. Even just changing our housing is difficult – but entirely possible. To do so we must realise that we need cultural change as much as technological and political change, and that we must ensure that those less well-off have just as much opportunity to prepare as the wealthy.

**www.leicesterexchanges.com**

## Mini glossary

**resilience** – *ability to cope; flexibility*

**refuge** – *a safe place*

# Activities

## Brainstorm

Brainstorm to find out what you know about potential solutions to the climate change problem.

1.  Write a definition for 'mitigation' and 'adaptation' in relation to climate change. What are the advantages and disadvantages of each?

    ........................................................................................................................................................................

    ........................................................................................................................................................................

2.  What do you know about the Kyoto Protocol? What is the aim of the Protocol?

    ........................................................................................................................................................................

    ........................................................................................................................................................................

## Oral activities

3.  In the article *Adapting to the greenhouse* on pages 16-17, it is suggested that poor people will be more vulnerable to the effects of climate change than wealthy people. Why do you think this might be? Discuss the issue in groups of four. You should think about: housing; agriculture; migration; dealing with natural disasters, and access to 'green' technology.

    NOTES...............................................................................................................................................................

    ........................................................................................................................................................................

    ........................................................................................................................................................................

4.  'This house believes that carbon offsets are an ineffective way of slowing global warming. They do not help to reduce our dependency on fossil fuels and merely create the illusion that governments and corporations are taking action to reduce their emission levels.' Debate this motion in two groups, with one group arguing in favour and the other against.

    NOTES...............................................................................................................................................................

    ........................................................................................................................................................................

    ........................................................................................................................................................................

## Moral dilemma

5.  You are updating the heating system in your house. You currently use gas but know that this is a significant contributor to global warming. You could have solar panels installed which would be much better for the environment, but would be quite costly and would affect the picturesque appearance of your home. What do you do?

# Activities

## Research activities

6. The Kyoto Protocol is just one agreement in the history of climate change negotiations. Find out about another legally binding agreement which was drawn up to help combat climate change. You can use the Internet and newspaper reports to help you. Write a brief summary of your findings.

   CONCLUSION ....................................................................................................................................................

   ....................................................................................................................................................

   ....................................................................................................................................................

7. Carry out a research project into the different ways countries are adapting to the effects of climate change. Use the Internet to find example of how communities around the world are altering their lifestyles in response to global warming. Are you surprised by any of your findings?

   NOTES ....................................................................................................................................................

   ....................................................................................................................................................

## Written activities

Complete the following activities in your exercise books or on a sheet of paper.

8. Read *We have to adapt culturally to climate change* on pages 24-25. Write a response to Dr Jenny Pickerill. Do you agree with her arguments that cultural changes need to be made in order to adapt to climate change? You can agree or disagree with some or all of her points, but make sure you support your views with valid reasons and evidence.

9. Imagine you have to teach a class of younger pupils about the different solutions to climate change. Write an entertaining poem or song to inform them of the various solutions available. It should keep them interested as well as emphasising the key points you want to get across.

## Design activities

10. Read *Key agreements in the history of climate change* on pages 22-23. On a large piece of paper, design an illustrated timeline showing the key events from the article in chronological order. You can include additional information on your timeline from your own research.

11. Design an advert for a wind power company which sells carbon offsets. The advertisement should be suitable for publication in a national newspaper and give readers detailed information on what carbon offsets are and why buying from a wind power company is particularly beneficial. You must also make sure the ad is eye-catching to encourage sales.

## Key Facts

▶ The Earth's climate has always changed naturally in the past. But what is happening now is potentially a big change in the Earth's climate, this time caused mainly by human activity. (page 1)

▶ How our climate will change depends on the future level of carbon dioxide and other gas emissions in the atmosphere. Some impacts are also highly unpredictable in a complex climatic system. (page 3)

▶ Climate change is likely to have far-reaching and catastrophic social impacts and will affect communities in different ways. (page 7)

▶ Changes in climate will impact on agriculture and food production in many ways. Production may increase with higher temperatures in middle and higher latitudes, since the length of the potential growing season may be increased. (page 8)

▶ The $CO_2$ released each year from forest loss is higher than that released by our yearly transport emissions. (page 10)

▶ One-third (33%) of the public now agrees with the statement 'it is not yet clear whether climate change is happening or not – scientists are divided on this issue', compared to only 25% in 2007. (page 12)

▶ It seems that most Britons also believe that politicians are not doing enough against global warming, with 73% agreeing with the statement 'there is no serious political will worldwide to tackle climate change'. (page 13)

▶ Mitigation needs international agreement and national enforcement; emissions from one country threaten everybody, and cutting them will take time. (page 16)

▶ The Kyoto Protocol was the world's first international agreement on how to tackle climate change, and an important tool that governments around the world have used since it was made law in 2005. (page 18)

▶ A carbon offset is a credit for greenhouse gas reductions achieved by one party that can be purchased and used to compensate (offset) the emissions of another party. (page 20)

▶ Adapting is sometimes suggested as the easier option than mitigating. Rather than fundamentally changing everything about how we live today, we could plan for a different future and increase our resilience to any changes ahead. (page 24)

▶ Housing – both in construction and use – consumes significant amounts of energy and contributes at least 25% of all carbon emissions in Britain. (page 25)

## Glossary

**Adaptation** – In relation to climate change, adaptation is the notion of responding to the effects of global warming by adapting our lifestyles to altered environments. Examples of adaptation include changing food production methods to accommodate altered growing seasons or building houses from materials which are able to withstand more extreme weather patterns.

**Carbon footprint** – A carbon footprint is a measure of an individual's effect on the environment, taking into account all greenhouse gases that have been emitted through heating, transport, lighting etc. throughout that individual's average day.

**Carbon offsets** – Carbon offsets are a reduction of greenhouse gas emissions made in order to compensate for greenhouse gas production somewhere else. A company may purchase carbon offsets in order to meet caps or regulations, without actually having to reduce their own emissions.

**Climate change** – Climate change describes a global change in the balance of energy absorbed and emitted into the atmosphere. This imbalance could be triggered by natural or human processes. It can cause either global or regional changes in weather averages and frequency of severe climatic events.

**Climate change refugees** – Also known as 'environmental migrants', climate change refugees are people who have been forced to leave their homes following severe changes in their local environment as a result of global warming.

**$CO_2$ emissions** – Carbon dioxide gas released into the atmosphere, for example when fossil fuels are burnt.

**Global warming** – A rise in global average temperatures, caused by high levels of greenhouse gases entering the atmosphere. Global warming is affecting the Earth in a number of ways, including melting the polar ice caps, which in turn is leading to rising sea levels.

**Greenhouse gases** – A greenhouse gas is a type of gas that can absorb and emit longwave radiation within the atmosphere: for example, carbon dioxide and methane. Human activity is increasing the level of greenhouse gases in the atmosphere, causing the Earth to warm.

**IPCC** – An abbreviation for the Intergovernmental Panel on Climate Change, the leading scientific body which reviews and assesses climate change research.

**Kyoto Protocol** – An international treaty which sets binding targets for 37 countries to reduce their greenhouse gas emissions. It was made international law in 2005 and was the world's first international agreement on tackling climate change.

**Mitigation** – In relation to climate change, mitigation refers to the act of reducing, or limiting, the level of greenhouse gas emissions entering the atmosphere in an attempt to slow the rate of global warming. Examples of mitigation include government emissions target campaigns and the development of 'greener' technology.